Joan Newmann was born in Tandragee, County Armagh, in 1942. She was educated at Portadown Technical College, Rupert Stanley College in Belfast, and, as a mature student, at Queen's University Belfast, where she graduated in 1981 with a BA in English. She has taught English at a number of secondary schools, has been a part-time tutor at the University of Ulster at Coleraine, and has also worked for the Workers' Educational Association. In 1992–3 she was writer-in-residence at the Verbal Arts Centre in Derry. She teaches creative writing in schools for The Arts Council of Northern Ireland and for the Pushkin Prizes Trust. She was a member of the Philip Hobsbaum Belfast Writers' Group and the Queen's University Festival published a pamphlet of her poetry, *First Letter Home*, in 1965. Since then her work has appeared in a wide variety of publications, including *Northern Review*, *Kilkenny Magazine*, *Honest Ulsterman*, *Women's News*, *Fortnight* and *Causeway*, as well as being broadcast on BBC television and radio.

Joan Newmann lives in Ballycastle, County Antrim. She is a member of the Word of Mouth Creative Writing Collective. *Coming of Age* is her first full collection.

Coming of Age

JOAN NEWMANN

THE
BLACKSTAFF
PRESS

BELFAST

ACKNOWLEDGEMENTS

Some of these poems have previously appeared in: *Causeway*; *Circumcision Party* (Honest Ulsterman pamphlet, 1994); *Exposure*; *First Letter Home* (Queen's University Festival pamphlet, 1965); *Fortnight*; *Full Moon*; *Honest Ulsterman*; *Interest*; *Kilkenny Magazine*; *Muse*; *Northern Review*; *Our Say*; *Ratpit*; *Suffer Little Children* (Diamond Poets pamphlet, University of Ulster at Coleraine, 1991); *Verse*; *The Wearing of the Black* (Blackstaff Press, 1974); *Women's News*; *Writing Ulster* (University of Ulster at Coleraine, 1991); and *Young Commonwealth Poets* (Heinemann, 1965).

First published in 1995 by
The Blackstaff Press Limited
3 Galway Park, Dundonald, Belfast BT16 0AN, Northern Ireland
with the assistance of
The Arts Council of Northern Ireland

© Joan Newmann, 1995

Typeset by Paragon Typesetters, Queensferry, Clwyd
Printed in Ireland by ColourBooks Limited

A CIP catalogue record for this book
is available from the British Library

ISBN 0-85640-487-X

for Kate

I look around at the walls, the window; it's the same, it hasn't changed, but the shapes are inaccurate as though everything has warped slightly. I have to be more careful about my memories, I have to be sure they're my own and not the memories of other people telling me what I felt, how I acted, what I said: if the events are wrong the feelings I remember about them will be wrong too, I'll start inventing them and there will be no way of correcting it, the ones who could help are gone.

MARGARET ATWOOD
from *Surfacing*
(André Deutsch, 1973)

CONTENTS

LOGOS

I am carried in a garden,
Fingers under my chin,
Spilling backwards, weight
Without strength.
Pinks, mauves, purples,
All the lupins growing
From buds in blue
To fleshy stems that hide
In wet brown earth.

An American soldier – smiling,
Squatting at eye level – feeds me
A long grey strip
Of chewing gum: 'Don't swallow it,
Honey, don't swallow it.' I smile,
Swallowing it, my gullet gagging.
Coloured in behind him,
Chewing, talking – blue pond,
Green grass, a yellow sun
Shining all about me.

THE HAND THAT ROCKS
for Mary Robinson

My uncle, the carpenter, finished the big cot
Painted in camouflage maroon and olive.

My mother's sisters brought water from the well,
Standing on a stool to reach the tea caddy.

They rock me, I loosen
To the swing and swing and
Rockers rhythmic sing
Staccato song on stone.

Tune whirrs to laughing.
I am clothed in many colours:
I am wadded wadding in the dark.
Wooden slats caged around me
Inside out, firelight licking.

TOUCH HAS A MEMORY
for Nicola

Wrapped in flame-warmed winceyette,
Bitter tang of vomit in my head,
Hammocked in my mother's lap,
Her knees spread wide to take me in.
Grey outside light
Burning in the window.

The blurred, furred sinews come at me.
Fire cat, live coal flickering your eyes.

I am floating in arms
Linked in loosely woven fingers,
Rocked to the rhythm of hearts.

PLANE SPOTTING

My uncle bringing it grey from the war,
A manual for pilots –
My first book.
So I could, from the circled undercarriage,
The engine's jar,
Tell friend from foe.

'Georgy, Porgy, pudding and pie' –
Coaxing my horse
The length of crooked potato drills
My aunts had dug;
Its wooden bench, flat head,
Left no place to hide.

Shiny pictures of the men
Helmeted for battle
Did not speak to me.
I talked to them.
I was I,
Free of what is truth and what is lie.

4

CARRIE

See us in the middle of the night:
My aunt crying as if in physical pain;
My uncle clearing the wardrobe,
Piling his suits on his bicycle;
Carrie and I emerging into the oil lamplight
Which moves from place
To place in angry hands.
We blink like guinea fowl
And are aware of our own
Bulk: finding it useless.
Straining to grip a word.
We'd never know. Mysterious things happen
Behind shut doors . . .
Carrie said, 'Anyone would be better anywhere.'

TO MORO

My mother saying there's Willie Thornton,
Meeting him, turning him, walking away.
I, kneeling on the couch, see them stare
Through the steamy windows of his car.
She returns, lifting a weed from the path,
Pausing too long at the door, avoids my aunt's face.
'He had it in the back – it's just a box.'
And I hear in my nerves a low raw roar.
My aunt plunges knuckles into eye sockets.
And forever the boy I fantasised with ginger hair,
A big, red baby.

She comes greyly down grey stones under a winter
    sycamore
And we have waited,
No one lighting the lamp
In the red–black heat of stove.
Her coat belt trails and her grey skin
Hides behind a bowed neck, a wreath of hair.
Nothing to say, crying that sounds like laughing
Filling hollows, and a cardboard box
Of baby clothes to be camphored in the wardrobe.

ROOKS
for Angela

Feather and soot, squawk and tumble,
Three young rooks in the empty fireplace.
We kept them in a box netted with wire,
Fed them hen meal from the back of a spoon.
Days of growing, fur bellies feathering.

Like a shot rook swinging,
I did not return.
Three heads that had cried with all their power,
Caught for ever in need, necks stretched,
Mouths full wide with want.

DUNKLE

With ducks on fly-crazy puddles
We expose feet too long webbed in leather,
Feel the warm slide of silt and slime,
Wriggle of life beneath our soles.
Unaware of the sun's swing
Until our laughter – hot smell of fermentation –
Brings mother-shouts of disbelief,
Sullying the place with names they could not say.

ONE TO ROT AND ONE TO GROW,
ONE FOR PIGEON, ONE FOR CROW

The gypsy passed me three times
Sunwise under the donkey's belly,
Pushing down my shoulders,
Forcing my face against acrid fur,
The tawny matted wool,
Inner thigh, sharp, restless hooves.

The gypsy, haloed in the sun,
Sure as the rhythm of the moon,
Knew that the sulky donkey,
Mucus by its shy eyes,
Would bear upon its back
The burden of my whooping cough.

GERANIUMS THE WORLD OVER SMELL THE SAME

Mrs Bradley's parlour of a Saturday evening,
I being told to go and play, sensing adult secrets;
And the long times when I squeezed the leaves of the
    pelargoniums,
Watching the drinkers and the flirters through the
    window;
The alcove with the scarlet blooms,
Their essence on my fingers repelling me.

ALL YOUR EGGS

'Mrs Greenlee hits people.'
I was used to peace
And pleasure.

This room had thirty strangers
Rolling plasticine: I coiled
And wove as I was wont to do
A basket of beauty – brown –
Perfect eggs in blue and white.

'Time's up.' And all creation
Pummelled together
In a clod.

I kicked the autumn earth
With my big brown school shoe.
This thing was lesser than the thing
I had: I knew.
My mother bit her lip as I explained
That I was never going back.

DAVY McDONALD THE ROADMAN

Davy McDonald used few words:
Broom whispered kerb's edge,
Shovel groaned stone on metal
Metal on stone, tipped grit
In heaps along the hawthorn hedge.

We sat on the bank,
Eating soda bread spread with butter,
Watching work winding with the road.

When Davy died the council wanted
To reclaim his brush and shovel,
Shafts worn shiny with the hug of his hands.
They rested in our shed.

SPLINTERS

Thundergrey stones in liquorice tar;
Dry, mute grasses still with heat;
My mother – blue teddy-bear coat
Striding against the bluer sky,
Wrath bursting in short-breath gasps.

'Get out of the way, the two of you,'
Edie shouted, taking my mother over.
Sylvie and I lay on Pearl's bed, red blanket stitching,
The weft and warp of army charcoal wool.

Joan Collins, Lana Turner, Doris Day smiled up
From this coarse background round the magic rectangle
Of Pearl's forbidden cigarette cards. I listened
For the voices of the women in the kitchen.

We sang, 'There's a pawnshop
Round the corner in Pittsburgh, Pennsylvania . . .'
Pencil in Pennsylvania
As thick as a telegraph pole
In the song in our heads.
Edie shouting not to wreck the beds.

A coolness – anger dead. My mother
Holding my hand without care

In the lateness of the darkening day,
'You're not to say where we went,' spat
In threat as I pulled ahead,
Seeing home.

POTATO GATHERING

As keen as the day
Brown earth turned on rusty stalks,
We bought from the field
Stones of potatoes. I stayed,
Bowing my back, soil in nails,
Breaking from the slow lifting rhythm
So potato flesh did not chafe on wire.
'Can she stay, Sam?' my mother promised to ask.
They queued for pay – I lingered,
Unrewarded, for my first work.

Esther McIlroy and Margaret Jelly,
Loud and linking arms, passed me,
Kneeling, hiding in the sheugh,
Tears that could not spill wetting my lips.

MARY VIOLATED

He had taken Mary, her shuttered eyes
Clicking open and open blue glass,
China head and hands and feet;
Limp, a body of stuffed cloth,
And with a lipstick scored on her,
I thought, buttocks and pubes.

I still see the shed –
Hear his laugh, a grown man,
Bobby Quinn,
His name comes back and know
The stain which stayed meant worse.

TWELFTH

Forty years ago in brand-new sandals
Running sponge-soled and clumsy,
Wanting to walk with the music and being
Trapped between my aunt's tight hand and the skin
Of a Lambeg drum;
Frayed cane beating on my solar plexus;
Stamen of orange lily; worn leather straps;
Bellying banner: nostrils clog
To the pulsing smell of other people's flesh,
Mustiness of the inside of other people's wardrobes.

FAITH MISSION

Smoke-black night settling in damp ditches.
Children, lagging, by the drifting drone
Of women's voices kept secure.

Dick McCullagh's hands hard
Push me onto last spring's moss,
Last summer's blackberry bramble,
My Sunday-school hat,
Elastic under chin sustains the shock.

He fells his weight to trap me; feel
My shoes sink in brackish water:
Screech nails on glass, ice in air,
To running feet.
'It was a joke – a bit of fun.
No need to shout. No need to shout!'
Silent, sodden, ashamed, I cannot see.

PINK KNICKERS

Landlocked children see the sea
One day a year;
Invaded by its gush,
Wary of its octopuses,
We run the length of sand
For consummation.

Tempting us out,
Startling us
With sudden violence
(A boy was drowned one year),
We withstand the ebb,
Confused and dripping,
Chastised.

A paper bag of buns
And bitter lemonade,
The taste of salt
Upon our lips.

New interlock knickers
Shocking as the flesh of salmon
Ballooned upon our pre-pubescent thighs.

PIG STICKING

Rotting apples hung in the air,
Rivulets of scummed and fly-high
Pig manure, young pigs squealing
– We were told to go away –
Cauldrons steaming on stilts.

'There he is now. The pig-killer.'
Uneasy afternoon, our play
Pierced by pig-shrieks –
Sharp, slicing through the closed barn doors.
'What's the boiling water for?'

River of red swilled into the yard.
Men came in to tea.
We went to see, stepping over
Blood clots caught in straw,
Carcasses gutted,
Stretched, scraped, shaved,
High-diving from hooks.
Poised in pirouette.

I carried home an enamel dish;
Unsliced livers gurgling softly,
Iron-smell, blood a tacky lukewarm gelatine
Drying on my fingers in the dark.

MAGGIE

It was always Friday
And there were brandy balls in a hand-soiled sugar bag,
And young peas in your garden that I'd flick with my
    tongue,
Hiding the pod in the long grass.
From the apple tree I could see you through the
    window making bread;
Later we would eat it dripping butter.
And there was a little glossy table
That ricketed on three legs,
A cascade of flowers dusting pollen on its polish.
And you, slow and shrewd and laughing.

I look at you now,
Seeing the black hollows of your dead nostrils,
The mauve tightening on your lips.

CATS AND LIES

My aunt
'The gypsies must have taken them.'
Their phantom caravans, ghostly piebalds,
Swarthy skin smoking over heathen fires,
Peopled the side roads of my fear.

My uncle
'I put them in a sack: flung them in the flax hole.'
Rushes rooted in liquid ranker than nightmare.
The fleshy splash: waste of breath.

My aunt lied
My uncle said
My uncle lied
My aunt said.

PETROSELINUM SATIVUM

My aunt holding a fistful against sick evening light
Seeping through window glass behind her: 'Boiled in
   a pint
Of new-drawn well water.' A tumblerful – dark
   brown liquid mud,
Smell of damp autumn vegetation
Rotting under winter grasses,
My palate cringing, my throat repelled.
'Drink it: drink it all: parsley for the kidneys,'
They chant, '– or is it celery?'

THE ANGEL OF DEATH

Mary Farquhar burst from the bus
Into our house of sickness.
We had suspended our lives
To let my mother breathe.

Mary Farquhar heard the slow croak,
The thwarted face, erratic heave
Of the patchwork quilt
And spoke of the death rattle.

Mary Farquhar slammed open
Sudden glass on worn sashes.
I escaped to the loanen,
Counting the frayed threads of my blazer:
Watching the open bedroom window
So I might know when to return.

STROKE

We stood at the end of the bed,
Feet soles sticking to the lino.

I look on the woman.
The tongue swollen, the eyes death-tight.
The paralysed jaw drawing the mouth
Upward on the right side.
Seven days and nights of moistening the lips
With glycerine on lint.

The eyes, unfocused, started open out of bone.
We cried the day she spoke:
'Away' – a million times – 'away, away.'

Coming back from death to learn to live again.
'For perhaps five years,' the doctor said.

THE WHEEL CHAIR
for Ruth Hooley

The house full of emptiness
Except for my mother, paralysed.
I signed the paper, primary six fat-loop;
Down the path it came – stiff brown wrapping;
Coarse, fuzzy, strong string.
'It's your wheel chair.' Its pieces
Piled on the bed higher than Christmas.

Saw with a sharp knife – its newness,
Unsat-on fawn corduroy, the gleam of promise in
    its chrome.
Finding a spanner, I tightened bolts,
Slotted foot rests, struggled with arm pads,
Forcing them into screw holes back to front.

My mother, tumbled to the bed's edge,
Little patience with the unyielding right arm,
Hurrying the shoes and stockings,
Her breath, fast and wheezing.
She fixes her hair with her left hand,
Tries to draw a comb through mine.
We fill the mirror – she dubious, I triumphant –
Behind us a chariot to let the world in.

I cannot wait; she is too slow.
She warns me not to hurt her.

We burst out – up the stony path –
I as proud as if pushing out a first-born –
Its wheels as bright and whirring
As a brand-new bicycle – slope
Straining me – we are on the road –
In the sky – at the grass – she says
We had better turn back for today.

It sat gathering our grime,
Shy and nervous like a badly broken foal,
Reminding her of her uselessness,
A body to be hid at home.
Me – of stunted possibilities,
Of pleasure thwarted,
Of feet that could still run.

LET'S PRAY

You weren't allowed to sing on Sunday afternoons
(Not songs, I mean, only hymns from Sunday school)
In the dry dead halls of the house.
And the father went to sleep, and we tried to play,
Half-hearted, every whisper shushed.

This Sunday was rolling rain-clouds and heaving leaves,
And James did something bad.
The father came to us, like God personified,
And struck and struck the cowering child.
'Please, please, dear Jesus, make him quit.'

By the stairs, a purple thunder sitting on the skylight,
And through the front-door glass, dark bride's blossom
Beat like teachers' canes against themselves.

'Suffer little children . . .' I croaked, not loud enough
For even me to hear,
And ran a race-pounding heart out of there, off home,
With God and God-men in every darkening hedge-hole,
Thrashing iron rods.

COMING OF AGE IN TANDRAGEE

'I had a pain and then it all just flowed away
Into the toilet.' We sat agog, studying
Sweat-stained, thread-sucked sewing,
As Ann McCracken told us what we were in for.

My initiation: a maroon blot on a friend's sheet,
Which I, in confusion, covered up.
Head and crazy stomach, the sun too light.
I, high on the leather saddle of their bike,
Was sent a mile and a quarter to buy
Three-quarters of a pound of chump steak.

At the day's end I
Could not forgive
The leak that would not stop,
The raw thing I'd become.

RUBY

Ruby led me to her bed –
Hard, dark utility furniture –
A sky thick as a burial.
I lay sombre, shocked
That a quarter of a mile
Through hazelnuts, blackberries,
Spongy meadow, flax hole and corn,
Our house howled with drawn blinds.
Ruby, awkward, lay beside me –
A brattle of thunder in the iron bedstead,
Lightning that could choose to carry us off.
I sat startled; Ruby, autumn in her hair,
Kneeled arranging scarves to mask the mirror.
Caught in the reflection I was stricken
By a glimpse of my mother's parting.

WESLEY

Years ago you dispensed with the niceties of socks
    and underwear.
I remember white flesh staring
From a rip in the seat of your dungarees.
And one Christmas you gave to me
A glass, slobber-marked, full of parsnip wine,
And a slice of apple pie on a cracked saucer,
Poured on cream, and were delighted when I ate it
With a little rusty spoon.

They say that you sit up all night:
That you never go to bed:
That you have no bed to go to.

Things have begun to rot
– The curtains at the windows –
And you come from the dark, cabbage-smelling
    kitchen
In an ex-army greatcoat
Like a mole.

You've even stopped your sacrificial kill
Of goat, which used to hang, fly-infested,
In the milk house.

And you'd eat at it for weeks,
Sent slices for the neighbours –
They threw it all away.

You shaved for my uncle's wake:
Bleeding pimples patched with newspaper,
Tears in your eyes.
Standing awkward in the kitchen with the women,
Cow dung the length of your wellingtons.

FIRST LETTER HOME

I miss the flagstone kitchen oozing cooling-cake smells,
And the shelf in the shed crawling rusty fungus.
The barrel underneath my bedroom window, spurting
   water blubbing from the spout.
A rug, rolled up and kept behind the door,
Unrolled on Fridays when the lamps were filled,
And the spilled paraffin stains and stink.
Even the dry lavatory – bucket and a wooden bench,
Squares of newspaper jabbed onto a nail,
And at the bottom of the garden – a disposal hole
That breathed out wisps of rankness on the hot, hot days.
My room, that always shed its paper in the winter,
And the bookcase staggering lopsided with the weight
Of books that were no use, that I could not throw away.
(I bet you burned them when I left.)
The baths on Saturdays before the darkening light and
   fluttering fire,
The bath, a chipped enamel basin (polythene of late),
Half-filled, and the kettle, sooty-bottomed, to reheat it.
It took so long to wash in sections, an hour perhaps . . .
I miss your kneeling down to soap my feet.

RAT'S LOT

Once, under a haystack, young rats,
Fat and pink, like uncooked cocktail sausages.
The farmer skewered them, warm and breathing, on
    a pitchfork.

There was an old griddle by the water-barrel,
Spread thick and slimy with birdlime.
I, a child, watched from a distance the stuck
    rat struggling.
Hunger-fury burned its eyes: the child threw cheese.
In the morning, rat was glued, mouth-down.

They kept it in a cage for three days;
It had learned to stop lurching against the wire,
To stop gnawing – and wait.
When the cage opened, it was too wise or too weak
    to move.
They prodded its convex back and it flew in fear.
Rat hadn't a chance – the terrier's jaws were waiting.

Rats come starving up from the river in winter;
Fill their bellies with oatmealish poisoning:
Back to the water, the first sip explodes them.

Rat-guts, flesh-pink and bloodless, skidded over a
    wet road.
Skin, like a child's sogged fur mitt; tail,
Bony, whippity, dead.

BETRAYAL

She thought of newts (sitting alone in the antiseptic
    room – waiting),
Of their arms and legs and splayed toes,
Faces old, like shrunken snakes; slats of eyes
Seeing right back to the tip of the thick tail.
Shallow, mud-coloured enclosure, and maybe
    thirty newts.
A shapeless one had lain by a chunk of hard plaster.
Newt embryo – no legs, no arms.
But how could such neuter things copulate!
'I must stop thinking of newts.'

The sofa was plush, and it stung her thighs.
Horsehair . . . Runyon used to wait for her in
    the paddock,
And the smell afterwards; especially of the hand that
    petted his slobbered mouth.
Runyon was sold to Sharkey, and she kept the
    slacks, unwashed,
And secretly she used to sniff at them.
On a push-bike in wet July, she had flown to see
    her horse.
But he didn't know her . . . perhaps it was just the
    bread all the time.

Two birds flew onto the windowsill: one, its
    wing-tips turned down,
The other, nonchalant, unmoved.
'Poor female thing.' She used to feel that way –
Wanting to crash into oblivion in a dark room
When Jack wanted only to play golf.
And Jack said golf would calm her nerves,
And she went, and hated the flat green and
    the symmetry,
The jokes, and the people in the bar.
And Jack said she was to try not to stare.

But the newts were still swimming in the water.
The sweet laziness of them.

She could hear the psychiatrist whistling down
    the corridor.
Jack had said that she mustn't tell *him* about the
    newts and Runyon.
Because *he* might think she was really ill.

LETTERS FROM THE ISLAND

The scrubland moistens round your feet at every
    spongy step,
And there's a cave under the south cliff
That thuds like a dull cannon to the lashes of the sea.
Over the slope, a baldy pebbled beach dragged by
    slimy seaweed.
You feel that if you cupped your hands to lift
The water, it would look a drowned grey-green.

A spring spurts peatish on the hill.
We've stood there, bare in the rain,
And laughed and sang the sea gulls hoarse.
And then we'd wander off apart –
Happy when we sought each other out.

And when we slept the day
And crouched, reading in the night,
Keeping lit the flur of turf, and brewing tea,
The paraffin-mellow glimmer burning at our eyes.

Just once there was a calmness in the sky,
When the ridge of pines stopped fighting.
And he talked his heart onto the moon.
There was no closeness that was close enough.

We tried to grind our bones into the rock –
To drown the gash of water throbbing in the cave
By our own hot gasps.

All night the wind and rain
Whee'd and oo'd around our shack.
He lit the lamp.
And I, in our warm cove of blankets,
Watched his naked shadow darkening the rafters.
Early in the weak washed light I try
To think the thoughts that move his sleeping face.

But the boat will come tomorrow.

RENTOKIL

A safe house.
At night, soft gargle of river darkness.
Pale light, comfrey, sunflowers
Higher than hedges, catching
A whistle of kingfisher turquoise,
Flash of salmon through ivied trees:
Heron, still on the weir;
Raw screech
Confirming our survival.

I, perching in the loft,
Mask filtering breath
Below stinging eyes.
Dripping from knotted pine,
Brown noxious liquid.

Twenty years later he happens to mention
Woodworm treatment may cause abortion.

WHEN LUCY CEASED TO BE

They found her dead, last Tuesday,
Straddled on a chamber,
Legs buckled in a terrible toilet-crouch.

The undertaker damped the pain-tensed face,
Pulled on the shroud over her clothes.
And while she lay, coffined in the kitchen,
Neighbours wept and stole her pots and pans.
Then wept again.

On Thursday afternoon the hearse broke down.
I hear you shout, 'By Christ, they'll not bury me
Out of a bloody black van!'

WORM

An earth of brown mud bearing down on you.
When I have a fever I always imagine coins, a heap
   of coins
Pouring out of a hole in the ceiling into a conical
   gold pile,
Pinning my hands and feet and smothering my throat.
Is it like that down there?

Stretched up, out, without clingers;
Chopped up by a sharp beak;

Wriggling about, blind little eyeless guts – living.
Jabbed on a hook.
Squirming with a barb through your belly.
Washed dead in a new wet world.

SCHIMMEL – A NICE WORD FOR AN
ENGLISH SPEAKER

Jane Taylor stepping to Tandragee,
Eighty years since she senses,
Shadowy and shifting white,
A horse, unbroken, human-shy,
Sinews straining, cross her path.

She turns and is knocked down by a motorcar,
Her black coat sucking brown road,
Whites of eyes strain to capture
The mirage, the shimmering.

White stallion rearing and hoofing:
White mare smothered, nostrils and lips
Clogged by an Indian blanket:
White horse chased to the cliff's edge
Shrieking and sliding; falling,
She strokes at the air.

They carry her, pale and perplexed,
To my grandmother's bed, her black
Felt hat waiting for a journey,
Her thick blond plait soaks with blood.

AT OSSIAN'S GRAVE
for Patrick Donohoe

You beside the Lagan, Patrick,
Me beside the Isis, arch
Swan pecking a dove-grey trusting cygnet.
It fears to come for bread.
Swans transmogrify into nurses' head-wear
Floating on a shallow sea of sleep.
Pain has become your second name.

'Boy Falls From College Roof.' The Oxford papers
Do not question: did he choose, from a bizarre
    perspective,
Dispassionate masonry, swallowing the cobbled path,
Withered grass, lurching heads of flowers, all his days
Dissolved in air?

Freesia perfume expectorating from watery stems
Catches you in the ether, dizzy jumble of hot noons,
Remembered laughter, arms outstretched,
Faery child, live light in your eye.

On Saturday I wrote 'By St Aldates':
'Quick brown bird under a yew
Spear the soft green body
Of the flailing caterpillar:

Wings will never open to pale damp dawn,
Blur of violet and vermilion . . .'
I did not know it was your requiem.

SORLEY BOY

Know that on Rathlin Island the boat pulls in,
Jarring on stone. Impotent on the mainland –
And that now, now, now,
Savage hands and slicing swords
Hack from me all I ever had.

No sorrow but my own,
A messenger hotfoot to say
The bloody deed is done –
Sniggers from behind court handkerchiefs.

Bladderwrack swirls in pools like woman's hair.
Sea birds persistent in their cry as babies.
Ocean drinking down pale horizon light.
I am stranded, screeching.

SERMON FOR THE BIRDS

Identifying you and the death you brought,
Hunch-winged, power centred in your legs,
Furtive lurking, jerking head, dipping and ripping.

The book showed you in silhouette
Ready to prey,
Crucified against an imaginary sky.
Paint did not reveal the glint of flint
That is your eye.

Majesty missing from your elevation,
The soft burden and your cruelty
Anchoring you.

Incongruous – beneath your own ruthless tail
The uncomprehending fan of the collared dove.

DEAR MARIETTA

Standing on a chair, 'She's tired.'
Shadows under thinking eyes
Reflecting the waves' build and fall.

Children cry when they are asked to rest:
Yours was a siren signifying pain
As your parents used the door to block the sun
And we walked.

We remember the first hot day of moving in:
You squatting, your grandmother sweeping sand
    on turds.
We have not forgotten what the eye saw.

Your third birthday: a proper cake –
It was nothing – the gifts, balloons,
Some words, a pair of purple trousers
And a jumper wild with animals.
It was nothing.

THE COMFORT OF SAINTS
for Mary Twomey

Mary, aghast with ache, spread
Her damp clothes on a dingy bush,
To bear the journeying: in remembrance
Blue flowers bloomed.

Brigid, finding no shrub,
Flung her cloak at a sunbeam.

And Gobnat, in fury at persistent evil
In her enemies, lulled a swarm
Of summer bees from thyme and clover
To sting the eyes and blur to blindness.

Kevin cupped his supplicatory hands,
Stilled with desire for vision.
A female blackbird, brown as the turf,
Nested there, rearing her fledglings
Before Kevin dared to move.

SEERS MUST SING
for Haris Vlavianos

Nazrul – famous Bengali poet –
In blotchy grey film he sings his song:
Musicians sing his song.
Though a Muslim, he wrote
Five hundred Hindu hymns:
The Hindus sing his song.
Professors intone his poetry;
A girl whirls to his music;
He writes on the evils of partition;
The country sings for Nazrul.

In '42, the year that I was born,
Nazrul tried in a recording studio
To talk to children and found
He could not speak
Nor ever did again.

The song of such prolific birds
Wavers, perhaps, grows fainter,
But does not merely stop.
In Europe fifty doctors could not fathom
What had coagulated in his head:
Some said syphilis,
Some said no, no,

'He liked the ladies but of course
He loved his wife.'
Nazrul clutching his boys in both arms,
Kamila in the background, bitter knowledge
Freezing in her eyes.

A film cameo: Kamila paralysed,
Stretched on her string bed;
Bewildered, speechless Nazrul squatting –
She struggles, scoops fingers full of rice,
Strains to place them in his mouth.
White grains drop on a whiter kurta.
Eviction, a hand about to thump the door.

Bangladesh before his death
Elevated him in their need for a Tagore.
He sits toothless and smiles just once
When he catches the hand
Of a young girl who is garlanding him.

HAPPY FAMILIES

My grandmother opened the door
To a worried child's face.
'Eliza, can you come, my mother's hurt?'
She went, untying her apron as she walked,
Talking to the boy who wanted her
To run. His mother, lying desperate and pained,
    ashamed,
'It's another one, Eliza' – through the children crying –
'And I jumped from the table.'

I thought of Sonia Tolstoy
As Leo was considering relinquishing the world,
Pregnant with her thirteenth child,
Vaulting the hedges in the garden
And hoping for the pain to start.

WEDDING NUPTIALS IN PLATANIA
for Stewart Parker

Walking musicians, sleeves rolled, lighting the place
   with music,
Moving to the unison of string and bow.
Sweets showered on the girl and boy
Parting the blocked streets of Platania.
Houses coloured like sugared almonds
Stuck on the edge of the mountain.

Precarious jubilation: I, a voyeur,
Trapped in the traffic, dulled and saddened by
   your dying,
Incredulous and privileged, witnessing
A procession circumambulating the same frieze
For hundreds and thousands of years.

You say, '*Na sas zeisoun*' – 'May they live for you' –
To the parents of the bride and groom.
I searched my head for the sound,
Formed it on my tongue and palate.
A woman – turned eyes
Dark with recollecting and forgetting,
Recognition of a foreign body,
A solitary traveller –
Cut through '*Na sas zeisoun*' with 'Fuck you.'

HER HAIR COILED BACK FROM HER
TROUBLED FACE

Jean Coleman surveyed the wide Atlantic
At eye level – her fingers limpets on the upturned boat –
The sea fleck and flash a purl and plain
Shrouding her, refusing release.
Her life always before her eyes,
This state was no surprise, no revelation.

But she could swim, they'll say.

Oh I could move in water

An ocean length of lung's air

Breathless, maybe never the shore

How to go down?

Maybe the sand – a gasp –

Begin again the endless tread.

Her life always before her eyes,
This state was no surprise.

MAN DANCING IN A LIGHTED WINDOW

He sways his arms in expansiveness,
Bends and unbends his knee; smiles at someone
Seated, whom we cannot see.
His body moves to music behind glass;
Strange magic of wordlessness.

Behind glass, darkness takes us: recalling
Mellow light, the man's tilted shining face,
Second of sublimation, dancing
For all he is worth.
The full of our minds –
That man beginning to dance
In a lighted room
Which could not draw its blinds.

FOR YASSER ARAFAT WITH LOVE

Lebanese boy in lighted khaki dancing
On planks; Cretan autumn moon
Swimming in fronds of tamarisk;
Boats wavering to the throb
Of underwater. Music fails.
The boy, vibrant as a young cedar,
Makes his feet move to a sound
Which is beyond us, at variance with sea,
Moment and movement, our breath
Stilled, fearing the endlessness; the end –
Comes down to the screak of wood
On the instant the music returns.

The Cretan town of Agia Galini sends a gift
For Yasser Arafat, a large mirror:
So that he may reflect on
A boy soldier dancing on turbulent water;
His own perturbed, unshaven face
Among the blue hand-painted perching doves.

LAST BOAT TO SPINALONGA

*I was used to seeing some of the tortured faces of the lepers,
but this time I was frightened. The new patient was a once
beautiful seventeen-year-old girl, not much above my own age,
and accompanying her were her parents. When I looked at her I
saw her skin all cracked and bruised, and the flesh open on her
head. The girl sat down inside the boat, and I was unable to
move from the hole at the rudder . . . That was the only place I
felt safe.*

Emmanuil Koukourakis, *The Island of Spinalonga*

Her father turning his head to the spray,
Knuckling water from his eyes;
A flat palm frantic to dry his face
Bright with straining
To do what was needed of him.
Her mother counting silently the bags,
Fingering her throat, and the evil eye
Pinned to her cardigan.

Coffins, square as fish crates,
For unconsecrated burial of the impure.
It did not do to say.

Sometimes a white bundle wrapped face and all
Against the rawness of it.

57

A newborn child who could be saved
If neither his mother nor his father
Moved to touch his flesh but bore him
In their memories and released him.

Water gulping at the boat's side,
Grain under varnish drowned to sight.
Sea, spilled turquoise ink, the sun beneath.
Counting time in the lap of the waves.
Every second the thread of a web
That the breath breaks.

PANAGIA
for Kate

You move behind stained glass
Opaque as ice eased from puddles
Held as melting precious in aching hands.

INGA

Journeying out in maps of all possible places
Brought you young and hopeful to our shore.

His long persuasive fingers under your armpits
Drawing your face towards intimate moss stitch:
Feet afloat on sphagnum gulping sudden fear:
Language leaving you, your throat tightening.

Scots pines, angry uncles impotent
In their yearning for the killing
Not to have been under their shelter.

Straggling summer flowers – honeysuckle, scabious,
    wild campion –
Incredulous cousins gaping and trembling.
Grasses sighing like distracted aunts.

Parent hills with the names of Knocklayd,
Carnanmore on them, linking
Arms in consolation in the glacial valley.
Pressing their sorrowing heads in cloud.

Far out on the bog in erica and sundew
A cluster of huge stones
With the hunched shoulders of grave diggers.

Your body among deep green and russet
Lying like a drift of unseasonal snow.

And the sea's untimely murmuring
Heilige Nacht . . . Heilige Nacht.

KORE

I am to come from darkness thick as sleep.
Sound – a keen ear held hard on drum-skin.
Eyes – irises stretched for lack of light.
Why should I fear his seeking, cleaving arms,
A bed fitting my shape, nesting our warmth?

To push upwards, sun burning blind-closed eyes –
Raw raucous screech of blundering brazen beast –
Thinness of air a-rush with crazy flight –
Stench of growth, fertility, flower –
I feel their desire to ask me to reveal
The way the earth will suck them in for time.

It takes me: pink anemones, blue irises,
Yellow poppies, borage, purple lupin,
Flap of white heron, water warm as blood,
My mother's house, its white bright walls,
Its turquoise blistered door, straight-backed chairs,
Onions, garlic, peppers, dripping olive oil;
Hands in the dance reach up to strangers' hands,
Feet leaving the ground – must I go down?

              My mother, Demeter;
King of the dark underworld, my husband:
I have no place between the two of them.